BEST. ANIMAL JOKES. EVER.

JOKES for KIDS

CHANTELLE GRACE

BroadStreet KIDS

BroadStreet Kids
Savage, Minnesota, USA

BroadStreet Kids is an imprint of
BroadStreet Publishing Group, LLC.
Broadstreetpublishing.com

Best Animal Jokes Ever

978-1-4245-6294-7
978-1-4245-6295-4 (eBook)

Design and typesetting | garborgdesign.com
Compiled and edited by Michelle Winger | literallyprecise.com

Printed in the United States of America.

21   22   23   24   25   26   7   6   5   4   3   2   1

CONTENTS

HOUND HYSTERIA

What happened to the dog that swallowed a firefly?

It barked with de-light.

Why don't dogs make good dancers?

Because they have two left feet.

When is a dog not a dog?

When it is pure bred.

What dog keeps the best time?

A watch dog.

What do you call a great dog detective?

Sherlock Bones.

What do you call young dogs who play
in the snow?

Slush puppies.

What type of markets do dogs avoid?

Flea markets.

When does a dog go "moo"?

When it is learning a new language.

How did the little Scottish dog feel when it saw a monster?

It was Terrier-fied.

Where do Eskimos train their dogs?

In the mush room.

What dog loves to take bubble baths?

A shampoodle.

Why do you get if you cross a chili pepper, a shovel, and a terrier?

A hot-diggity-dog.

What did the dog say when it sat on sandpaper?

"Ruff."

What do dogs eat at the movies?

Pupcorn.

What did the Dalmatian say after eating dinner?

"That hit the spot."

What is a dog's favorite dessert?

Pupcakes.

What do you do if your dog chews a dictionary?

Take the words out of its mouth.

How do you say goodbye to a curly-haired dog?

"Poodle-oo."

Why did the poor dog chase its own tail?

It was trying to make ends meet.

How are dogs like phones?

They have collar IDs.

CAT COMEDY

What do cats eat for breakfast?

Mice Crispies.

What does a twenty-pound mouse say to a cat?

"Here kitty, kitty, kitty."

What is a cat's favorite color?

Purrple.

What animals are the best pets?

Cats, because they are purrfect.

What are caterpillars afraid of?

Doggerpillars.

What's worse than raining cats and dogs?

Hailing taxis.

What kind of cats like to go bowling?

Alley cats.

What do you call a pile of kittens?

A meowntain.

What is a cat's favorite song?

Three Blind Mice.

What is it called when a cat wins a dog show?

A cat-has-trophy.

Why are cats so good at video games?

Because they have nine lives.

What's a cat's favorite dessert?

Chocolate mouse.

What do you call a cat wearing shoes?

Puss in boots.

Why do cats always get their way?

They make a purrsuasive case.

What do you call a cat that's in trouble with the police?

A purrpetrator.

What kind of sports cars do cats drive?

Furarris.

ARCTIC AMUSEMENT

Who is the penguin's favorite Aunt?

Aunt Arctica.

What's white, furry, and shaped like
a tooth?

A molar bear.

What's a penguin's favorite salad?

Iceberg lettuce.

Why did the penguin cross the road?

To go with the floe.

Where do penguins go to the movies?

At the dive-in.

How does a penguin make pancakes?

With its flippers.

Where do polar bears vote?

The North Poll.

Where do penguins go to dance?

The snow ball.

What do penguins have for lunch?

Icebergers.

Why don't you see penguins in the United Kingdom?

Because they're afraid of Wales.

How does a penguin build its house?

Igloos it together.

What do you get when you cross a walrus with a bee?

A wallaby.

How do penguins drink?

Out of beakers.

What do penguins wear on their heads?

Ice caps.

What do you get when you cross a penguin and an alligator?

I don't know, but don't try to fix its bow tie.

SEA LIFE SHENANIGANS

What does a shark like to eat with peanut butter?

Jellyfish.

What do you get when you cross fish and an elephant?

Swimming trunks.

How many tickles does it take to make an octopus laugh?

Ten-tickles.

What is a shark's favorite sci-fi show?

Shark Trek.

Why is a fish easy to weigh?

Because it has its own scales.

What do you call a solitary shark?

A lone shark.

What fish only swims at night?

A starfish.

Why are there some fish at the bottom of the ocean?

Because they dropped out of school.

Why don't sharks like fast food?

Because they can't catch it.

What do you call a fish without an eye?

A fsh.

What did the shark say to the whale?

"What are you blubbering about?"

Where do fish sleep?

On a seabed.

What is the strongest creature
in the sea?

A mussel.

Where do fish go when their things
go missing?

The Lost-and-Flounder Department.

How do oysters call their friends?

On shell phones.

What's the difference between a guitar and a fish?

You can't tuna fish.

Why do fish live in saltwater?

Because pepper makes them sneeze.

What do fish do at football games?

They wave.

Why did the fish blush?

It saw the ocean's bottom.

What does a fish do in a crisis?

Sea-kelp.

Okay that's enough fish puns.

It's time to scale back.

JUNGLE JEST

What kind of key opens a banana?

A monkey.

Why do gorillas have big nostrils?

Because they have big fingers.

How does a lion greet the other animals in the field?

"Pleased to eat you."

Why did the monkey like the banana?

Because it had appeal.

Why don't you have to tell an elephant a secret more than once?

Because elephants never forget.

Why didn't the boy believe the tiger?

He thought it was a lion.

What did the banana say to the monkey?

Nothing. Bananas can't talk.

Why are elephants so wrinkled?

They take too long to iron.

What kind of jungle cat is no fun to play games with?

A cheetah.

What do monkeys do for laughs?

They tell jokes about people.

How do you get down off an elephant?

You don't, you get down off a duck.

When is a well-dressed lion like a weed?

When he's a dandelion.

What sport don't you want to play with an elephant?

Squash.

Where do chimps get their information?

From the ape vine.

How do you raise a baby elephant?

With a forklift.

How do monkeys get down the stairs?

They slide down the bananaster.

Why are elephants so poor?

Because they work for peanuts.

What animal gets in trouble at school?

The cheetah.

What's black and white and blue?

A sad zebra.

Why can't a leopard hide?

Because he's always spotted.

Why did the elephant stay in the airport?

It was waiting for its trunk.

FARM FUNNIES

What do you get if you cross a chicken with a cow?

Roost beef.

What do you get from a pampered cow?

Spoiled milk.

What type of horses only go out
at night?

Nightmares.

What do you get when a chicken lays
an egg on top of a barn?

An eggroll.

What did the pony say when it had
a sore throat?

"I'm a little hoarse."

Why can't you shock cows?

They've herd it all.

Why didn't the chicken cross the road?

Because there was a KFC on the other side.

Why did the boy stand behind the horse?

He thought he might get a kick out of it.

What do you get when you cross a sheep and a honeybee?

Baahumbug.

What do you call a dancing sheep?

A baallerina.

What do you give a sick horse?

Cough stirrup.

What do you call a sheep that is always quiet?

A shhhheep.

Why did the pig become an actor?

Because he was a ham.

Why did the chicken cross the road?

To show everyone he wasn't chicken.

What kind of pigs know karate?

Pork chops.

What kind of ties do pigs wear?

Pigsties.

How do Hispanic sheep say
Merry Christmas?

"Fleece Navidad."

How many sheep does it take to knit
a sweater?

Don't be silly; sheep can't knit.

What do you call cattle with a sense
of humor?

Laughing stock.

What animal sounds like a sheep but isn't?

A baaboon.

Why was the sheep pulled over on the freeway?

Because she did a ewe turn.

What do you get if you cross an angry sheep and a grumpy cow?

An animal that's in a baad moood.

How do chickens bake a cake?

From scratch.

What do you call a cow with two legs?

Lean beef.

What do you give a sick pig?

Oinkment.

What do you call a cow with no legs?

Ground beef.

Why did the piece of gum cross
the road?

It was stuck to the chicken's foot.

What do you get if you cross a cocker
spaniel, a poodle, and a rooster?

"Cockerpoodledoo."

If fruit comes from a fruit tree, where
does chicken come from?

A poultree.

Where do hamsters come from?

Hamsterdam.

Why was the cow afraid?

He was a cow-herd.

What do you call a cow that just had a baby?

Decalfinated.

Where do milkshakes come from?

Nervous cows.

What do you call a sleeping cow?

A bulldozer.

What do you call a cow spying on another cow?

A steak out.

What did the teacher say when the horse walked into the class?

"Why the long face?"

What did the horse say when it fell?

"I've fallen and I can't giddyup."

What goes, "Oooooooo."

A cow with no lips.

What did the mama cow say to the baby cow?

"It's pasture bedtime."

How do horses stay in such great shape?

They keep a stable diet.

What day do chickens fear the most?

Fryday.

Why did Mozart get rid of his chickens?

They kept saying, "Bach, Bach!"

FOREST FOOLERY

How do bears keep their den cool
in summer?

They use bear conditioning.

Why was the rabbit so upset?

It was having a bad hare day.

What do you call a bear with no teeth?

A gummy bear.

What has 12 legs, six eyes, three tails, and can't see?

Three blind mice.

How do you know that carrots are good for your eyesight?

Rabbits never wear glasses.

What do you call a bear with no ear?

B.

What is an owl's favorite subject?

Owlgebra.

Why are teddy bears never hungry?

They are always stuffed.

What's gray, squeaky and lives in caves?

Stalagmice.

What do you call an owl with a deep voice?

A growl.

How do you save a deer during hunting season?

You hang on for deer life.

What do you get if you cross a bear with a pig?

A teddy boar.

Why did the owl say, "Tweet, tweet"?

Because she didn't give a hoot.

What is a baby owl after it is six days old?

Seven days old.

Why do male deer need braces?

Because they have buck teeth.

How do rabbits stay in shape?

They do a lot of hareobics.

How do you catch a squirrel?

Climb up a tree and act like a nut.

How can you tell which are the oldest rabbits?

Just look for the gray hares.

Who did Bambi invite to his birthday party?

His nearest and deerest friends.

How do mice feel when they are sick?

Mouserable.

What do you call a wet baby owl?

A moist owlette.

What do you call a bear caught in the rain?

A drizzly bear.

What kind of book does a rabbit like to read?

One with a hoppy ending.

Why did the owl invite its friends over?

It didn't want to be owl by itself.

Where do mice park their boats?

At the hickory dickory dock.

What did the judge say when the skunk came into his courtroom?

"Odor in the court."

POND PLAY

What happens when a frog parks in a no-parking space?

It gets toad away.

What do you call a crate of ducks?

A box of quackers.

What is a frog's favorite exercise?

Jumping jacks.

Who stole the soap?

The robber ducky.

Why are frogs so happy?

They eat whatever bugs them.

What do you get when you cross a frog and a bunny?

A ribbit.

What animal has more lives than a cat?

Frogs. They croak every night.

What did the duck say when buying lipstick?

"Put it on my bill."

What did one frog say to the other?

"Time is fun when you're having flies."

What time does a duck wake up?

At the quack of dawn.

What is a frog's favorite music?

Hip hop.

What do you get if you cross a frog and a dog?

A croaker spaniel.

What happens when a duck flies upside down?

It quacks up.

What is a frog's favorite hot drink?

Hot croak-o.

What goes dot-dot-croak,
dot-dash-croak?

A morse toad.   .

Which animal grows down?

A duck.

What do ducks watch on TV?

Duckumentaries.

What do you call a frog with no hind
legs?

Unhoppy.

Where do frogs leave their hats and coats?

In the croakroom.

What do you call a duck who leads an orchestra?

A conducktor.

What is a frog's favorite cold drink?

Croak-a-cola.

What does a duck like to eat with soup?

Quackers.

What do frogs wear on their feet?

Open toad shoes.

What did the duck wear to his wedding?

A duxedo.

What do you get when you cross a frog and a popsicle?

A hopsicle.

What do you get if you cross fireworks with a duck?

A fire quacker.

CREEPY CAPERS

What snakes are found on cars?

Windshield vipers.

Why did the snake cross the road?

To get to the other ssside.

What do you get when you cross
a snake and a pastry?

A pie-thon.

Why are snakes hard to fool?

You can't pull their leg.

What do you call a snake with a great
personality?

A snake charmer.

What do you call an alligator with a spy glass?

An investigator.

What is a snake's favorite school subject?

Hissstory.

What do you call a thieving alligator?

A crook-o-dile.

How do bees get to school?

By school buzz.

Two flies are on the porch. Which one is an actor?

The one on the screen.

What is the biggest ant in the world?

An elephant.

Why didn't the butterfly go to the dance?

Because it was a moth ball.

When did the fly fly?

When the spider spied her.

What do you call two ants that run away to get married?

Antelopes.

How do fleas travel from place to place?

They itchhike.

What is an insect's favorite sport?

Cricket.

Why did the kid throw the butter out the window?

To see the butterfly.

What kind of fly has a frog in its throat?

A hoarse fly.

Why was the bee's hair sticky?

Because it used a honeycomb.

SOARING SILLIES

What's yellow, weighs 1,000 pounds, and sings?

Two 500-pound canaries.

Where does a peacock go when it loses its tail?

A retail store.

Why does a flamingo stand on one leg?

> *Because if it lifted that leg off the ground, it would fall down.*

What kind of bird can carry the most weight?

> *The crane.*

Did you hear the story about the peacock?

> *It's a beautiful tale.*

What bird is with you at every meal?

> *A swallow.*

What do you give a sick bird?

Tweetment.

Why do birds fly south for the winter?

Because it's too far to walk.

Why do hummingbirds hum?

Because they forgot the words.

What bird is always sad?

The blue jay.

What's noisier than a whooping crane?

A trumpeting swan.

What do you call a bird in the winter?

Brrrd.

What do you get if you cross a canary and a 50-foot-long snake?

A sing-a-long.

What do you get when you cross a parrot and a shark?

A bird that talks your ear off.

What do you get when you cross a snowman with a vampire bat?

Frostbite.

Why did the canary sit on the ladder to sing?

It wanted to reach the high notes.

Why did the birdie go to the candy store?

It wanted a tweet.

Why do seagulls fly over the sea?

*Because if they flew over the bay,
they would be bagels.*

HINKETY PINKETY

Wouldn't it be funny if
we called a bumblebee a *fuzzy buzzy?*
Or a hippo a *floatie bloaty?*
A parrot could be a *wordy birdy,*
and a cat a *furry purry.*
If a dog were a *fluffy ruffy,*
a beluga could be a *pale whale,*
and a wasp a *wingy stingy.*

Your pet caretaker, or *critter sitter,*
would make for a happier dog—
a *merrier terrier* or a *jolly collie.*
A miniature sausage dog,
we'll call it a *teeny weenie,*
takes a bath and becomes a *soggy doggy,*

then lets out a bark or other *hound sound*.
That awakens the clever cat, or *witty kitty*,
who licks her paw warmer, her *kitten mitten*,
and begins searching for the rodent home,
aka *mouse house*,
and hopes for the chubbiest member,
the *fat rat*, to come out.
Sometimes the other rodent,
the *mouse spouse*, peeks its head out.
But most of the time,
it's the bushy-tailed spin, or *squirrel twirl*,
outside that catches the cat's eye.

When the slippery fowl, *slick chick*,
is up to her tricks,
you'll see another bird frown.
That's an *owl scowl*.
The runaway honker is a real *loose goose*.
It speeds past a lazy black bird, the *slow crow*,
and rushes by the casual parrot, or *walkie talkie*.
A royal raptor, *regal eagle*, takes to the skies
while pink birds chatter using *flamingo lingo*,
and the math-loving pelican, or *nerdy birdy*,
keeps an eye out for a sushi plate—a *fish dish*.
A quick dip in the water requires a bird dryer,
like an *owl towel*.

The sea lion should sign a contract, a *seal deal*,
with the hammerhead tattletale, the *narc shark*.
The blue-green moray, or *teal eel*,
could borrow the sea cow's mirror,
the *manatee vanity*,
to check his patient's arctic tooth—
polar molar.

A wheeled reptile might prefer to be labeled
a *skater gator*,
and it may have to dodge a tortoise
obstacle, or *turtle hurdle,* along the way.
Hopefully if it runs into a snowstorm,
a *lizard blizzard*,
it would take time to rest—*snake break*.
A magical reptile, or *wizard lizard*,
could turn a tool, a *snake rake*, into a shovel,
and hand it to an energetic hisser,
or *hyper viper*.

If you come across a cow stealer,
you might call him a *beef thief*.
At the same farm, you may encounter
a fake horse, or *phony pony*.
Of course, there's the hog with the
hairpiece, the *pig wig*,
and that super frugal lamb—*cheap sheep*—

with an unpleasant odor or *ewe pew*.
They all need the help of a lawful bird,
a *legal eagle*,
who sometimes wears a pest suit, or
mosquito tuxedo.

In the forest, a hare comedian,
the *funny bunny*,
sticks to its routine, or *rabbit habit*.
The mink offspring, *otter daughter*,
prefers to use the art stand,
the *weasel easel*,
to capture a marvelous marsupial—
the *awesome possum*.
Meanwhile, in the smelly animal bed,
or *skunk bunk*,
lies the mohawked stinker, the *punk skunk*,
who has stolen the canine's footwarmers,
or *fox socks*.

The spicy feline, *peppered leopard*,
fixes a cat sandwich, or *cheetah pita*,
and pours a drink into a long-necked
pitcher—a *giraffe carafe*.
That attracts the chubby chimp,
the *chunky monkey*,

who races over in a ring-tailed sportscar,
or *lemur beamer*,
leaving the cream-colored ape,
vanilla gorilla, behind.
On the way, it passes a sad wildebeest,
a *blue gnu*,
and an emotional feline, a *cryin' lion*.
What a wild mess—a real *jungle bungle*!

TITLE TRICKS

Hot Dog

> *by Frank Furter*

Cry Wolf

> *by Al Armist*

Sea Birds

> *by Al Batross*

Beekeeping

by A. P. Arry

I Like Fish

by Ann Chovie

Turtle Racing

by Eubie Quick

Off to Market

by Tobias A. Pigg

Mosquito Bites

by Ivan Itch

Desert Crossing

by I. Rhoda Camel

Those Funny Dogs

by Joe Kur

Crocodile Dundee

by Ali Gator

Let's Do That Now

by Igor Beaver

Animal Illnesses

by Ann Thrax

Equine Leg Cramps

by Charlie Horse

Smashing Lobster

by Buster Crabbe

The Unknown Rodent

by A. Nonny Mouse

Snakes of the World

by Anna Conda

A Whole Lot of Cats

by Kitt N. Caboodle

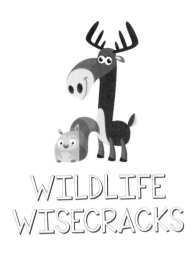

WILDLIFE WISECRACKS

If you're looking for great animal puns,

paws what you're doing and read these.

Raining cats and dogs is ok, as long as it doesn't...

reindeer.

The dad buffalo was sad when his male child left for college.

His parting words were,

"Bison."

Someone told me to get along little doggy,

so I bought a dachshund.

It was okay that the dolphin made a mistake.

He said he didn't do it on...

porpoise.

At first I wondered why cows had hooves instead of feet,

but then I realized it's because they...

lactose.

Crabs never give to charity because they are...

shellfish.

The veterinarian was sad when the monkey cut off its tail.

She said,

"It won't be long now."

An elephant stopped in the middle of telling a story...

never mind; it's irrelephant.

After the fish proposed an idea, he concluded with,

"Let minnow what you think."

The embarrassed bird of prey fell off a tree branch in front of a bunch of other birds.

It was really hawkward.

I find puns about pigs a little...

boaring.

The bird got arrested for stealing from the doctor.

What it was doing was...

ill-eagle.

It was strange to see the panda in a tank top.

But he does have the right to...

bear arms.

Someone said I sounded like an owl.

"Who?"

I asked everyone what happened to the lost cattle.

Nobody's herd.

The biggest goal of the detective duck was to...

quack the case.

The pig lied about taking a bath.

The farmer said, "Hogwash."

So it did.

Simba was walking too slowly so I told him to...

Mufasa.

Why isn't a koala a bear if he has all the necessary...

koalifications?

When you're down in the sea and an eel bites your knee...

that's a moray.

The farmer called the cow with no milk an...

udder failure.

It was raining cats and dogs when I walked outside.

I stepped in a poodle.

I saw a cow on stilts the other day.

The steaks have been raised.

If there's a problem at the beaver dam,

get otter here.

Whenever we go sightseeing in the ocean,

I find myself saying,

"Whale, hello there."

If a prize is won for coming in last,
tortoises are...

turtley the best.

Did you hear about the bear anarchy?

It was a pandamonium.

Sea lions love surfing?

That's the sealiest thing I've ever heard.

I tried to get the dog to bark,
but it was a...

hush puppy.

All those people out there wanting to
swim with the sea cows?

Oh, the humanatee.

I don't remember the specifics,
but Pavlov's theory...

rings a bell.

Board meetings with horses are useless.

They always vote neigh.

That owl does magic tricks?

It must be Hoodini.

I was shocked when a chicken ordered a drink at Starbucks.

It must have been an...

eggspresso.

Boring bees are annoying.

They drone on and on.

Dogs at a construction site are best at...

roofing.

Sometimes the best way to
communicate with fish is to...

drop them a line.

A man was hospitalized with six plastic
horses in his stomach.

The doctor said his condition was...

stable.

When you go on a safari,
take a good book.

Then you can read...

between the lions.

Australian bears hang out in trees together.

Their love language is...

koalaty time.

I thought I would like deer hunting, but I realized in the end I wasn't really...

fawned of it.

I caught a blue marlin.

I should probably listen to this fish.

It has a point.

I don't see what the big deal is about the black bird.

But people keep...

raven.

The lion exhibit at the zoo is quite popular.

I guess it's the...

mane attraction.

I don't know why people don't laugh at the large deer.

I find him pretty...

amoosing.

The prairie dog is really no big deal.
He's a...

meerkat.

The orca is an amazing actor.
It does a...

killer whale impersonation.